DOGS SET IX

POMERANIANS

Joanne Mattern

ABDO Publishing Company

visit us at
www.abdopublishing.com

Published by ABDO Publishing Company, 8000 West 78th Street, Edina, Minnesota 55439. Copyright © 2012 by Abdo Consulting Group, Inc. International copyrights reserved in all countries. No part of this book may be reproduced in any form without written permission from the publisher. The Checkerboard Library™ is a trademark and logo of ABDO Publishing Company.

Printed in the United States of America, North Mankato, Minnesota.
062011
092011

♻ PRINTED ON RECYCLED PAPER

Cover Photo: iStockphoto
Interior Photos: Alamy pp. 9, 19; Corbis p. 15; Getty Images pp. 6, 11;
    iStockphoto pp. 7, 13, 17, 18, 21; Photo Researchers p. 5

Editors: Megan M. Gunderson, BreAnn Rumsch
Art Direction: Neil Klinepier

Library of Congress Cataloging-in-Publication Data

Mattern, Joanne, 1963-
 Pomeranians / Joanne Mattern.
    p. cm. -- (Dogs)
 Includes index.
 ISBN 978-1-61714-992-4
 1. Pomeranian dog--Juvenile literature. I. Title.
 SF429.P8.M38 2012
 636.76--dc22
                        2011009546

CONTENTS

THE DOG FAMILY

Dogs and people have been friends for thousands of years. Today, dogs remain one of the most popular pets around the world. In the United States alone, there are more than 75 million dogs!

With more than 400 **breeds**, dogs come in all shapes, sizes, and colors. Yet, scientists have shown they all descended from the gray wolf. Dogs belong to the family **Canidae**. This name comes from the Latin word *canis*, which means "dog."

Today, dogs help people hunt and herd. Some guard property and keep people safe. Yet others don't perform difficult work. Instead, their job is to be good friends and pets. One of these companion breeds is the Pomeranian, or Pom.

It may be hard to imagine, but tiny Pomeranians have ancestors that were Icelandic sled dogs!

POMERANIANS

The Pomeranian is named for the historic region of Pomerania. Today, this area is part of Germany and Poland. The Pom belongs to a family of dogs known as the Spitz group. Originally, Spitz dogs were used for **drafting**, herding, and companionship.

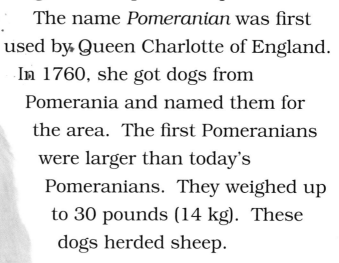

The name *Pomeranian* was first used by Queen Charlotte of England. In 1760, she got dogs from Pomerania and named them for the area. The first Pomeranians were larger than today's Pomeranians. They weighed up to 30 pounds (14 kg). These dogs herded sheep.

Spitz *is German for "sharp point."*

England's Queen Victoria imported some smaller Poms from Italy in 1888. She showed the dogs in England, and they won top honors. Because of the queen's influence, many people fell in love with the smaller-sized dogs.

That same year, the **American Kennel Club (AKC)** recognized the Pomeranian. This small **breed** is part of the AKC's toy group.

Charming Poms are happiest when spending time with their people.

WHAT THEY'RE LIKE

For such a small dog, the friendly Pomeranian has a lot of energy! This happy, intelligent **breed** loves to be with its family. It enjoys playing games, learning new tricks, and taking walks. Rough play can be dangerous for this tiny breed. So, the Pom should always be watched around small children.

Poms may be small, but they have big personalities! They are loyal to their owners and protective of their homes. Poms are not **aggressive**, yet these courageous animals make good watchdogs.

With Poms, barking comes with the territory. These dogs feel they have much to tell their families!

Pomeranians love to please their owners and are highly trainable. Agility training is a great way to bond with your Pom and provide regular exercise.

Your Pom may learn to bark less with proper training.

It is important that your Pom be well trained and taught who is the boss. Otherwise, you may find yourself living with your pet's demands!

COAT AND COLOR

Pomeranians have a variety of coat colors. Orange and red are the most popular. Brown, cream, black, and blue are other common colors. Poms can also have black and tan, **brindle**, or **parti-color** coats.

The Pomeranian's double coat protected its ancestors from northern Europe's cold, snowy winters. The undercoat is thick and soft. The outer coat is long, straight, and coarse. The Pom also has a thick frill of fur around its neck, shoulders, and chest.

The Pom's fluffy double coat **sheds** all year long. So, owners need to groom their dogs often. This will prevent the coat from getting tangled or **matted**.

The Pomeranian's distinctive full coat requires a real commitment from owners to keep it healthy and beautiful.

Size

Underneath all that fur, Pomeranians are very small dogs. Male and female Poms usually weigh between three and seven pounds (1.4 and 3.2 kg). The ideal weight for the **AKC** is between four and six pounds (1.8 and 2.7 kg).

The Pom's body is short and compact. Its straight legs end in small feet. A fluffy tail lies flat on the dog's short back. This is one of the **breed**'s best-known features.

A Pom's round head tapers to a short **muzzle**. Small, pointed ears sit high and erect. Beneath them, dark, almond-shaped eyes look around actively. The Pom's expression is often compared to that of a fox!

Although they are tiny, Poms see themselves as big and brave.

CARE

Pomeranians do not need a lot of exercise. But, they are very curious and energetic dogs. Poms will grow bored and unhappy if they are left alone for long.

A Pomeranian's coat needs a lot of care. These dogs should be brushed every few days. Whenever you groom your dog, its eyes and ears should also be cleaned. Also brush your dog's teeth at least once per week. This is important because Pomeranians are inclined to have dental problems.

There is another way to make sure your Pom stays healthy. See a veterinarian at least once a year. He or she will give your dog **vaccines**. At six months, the veterinarian will also **spay** or **neuter** dogs that are not going to be **bred**.

With their Spitz background, Pomeranians are usually hardy dogs. Yet like other toy **breeds**, they do have some health problems. They may have heart, breathing, or knee problems. Some Poms also suffer from skin infections.

Regular visits to a veterinarian will help you prevent and monitor health problems.

FEEDING

Pomeranians need high-quality food to stay healthy and active. Dry, canned, or semimoist foods are all options for this **breed**. A veterinarian or a breeder can suggest the best diet for your dog.

Be sure your Pom's diet helps it maintain a healthy weight. A tiny Pom cannot eat a huge meal. It may not be able to consume enough **nutrition** in just one daily meal. So, most adult Poms eat two or three small meals each day.

Like all dogs, Pomeranians need water to stay healthy. Dog owners should always have a bowl of clean, fresh water for their pets to drink. Extra water during hot weather or after exercise is especially important.

Bright eyes, a shiny coat, and lots of energy are evidence of a well-fed Pomeranian.

Things They Need

Are you getting ready to bring home a Pomeranian? It is best to have everything the dog needs before its arrival. Poms like to have fun and are curious about everything! These playful dogs enjoy having a lot of different toys to play with.

Like other dogs, your Pom will need grooming tools and food and water bowls. A comfortable bed will give your Pom a safe place to sleep. You will also need to get a collar with license and identification tags. A harness

and leash combo may work best for taking your Pom on walks.

Obedience training is important to commit to. Pomeranians need to know that their owner is in charge. They also need to learn how to behave at home and around other people and animals.

Due to their small size, Pomeranians can go almost anywhere with their owners! Always handle them with care and keep their safety in mind.

PUPPIES

Pomeranians are **pregnant** for about 63 days. A female Pom usually has a small **litter** of two or three puppies.

At birth, Pomeranian puppies are very tiny. They cannot see or hear until they are a few weeks old. They have to stay with their mother until they are six to eight weeks old. Then, they can be adopted. Healthy Pomeranians can live between 10 and 15 years.

It is important to **socialize** Pomeranian puppies. Owners should introduce their dogs to lots of new people, places, and animals. This helps Pom puppies learn about the world around them. Happy Pomeranians make wonderful best friends!

Take the time to provide your Pom pup with the love and care it needs and deserves. This will keep your new friend happy and healthy for years to come!

GLOSSARY

aggressive (uh-GREH-sihv) - displaying hostility.

American Kennel Club (AKC) - an organization that studies and promotes interest in purebred dogs.

breed - a group of animals sharing the same ancestors and appearance. A breeder is a person who raises animals. Raising animals is often called breeding them.

brindle - having dark streaks or spots on a gray, tan, or tawny background.

Canidae (KAN-uh-dee) - the scientific Latin name for the dog family. Members of this family are called canids. They include wolves, jackals, foxes, coyotes, and domestic dogs.

draft - the act of moving loads by drawing or pulling.

litter - all of the puppies born at one time to a mother dog.

matted - forming a tangled mass.

muzzle - an animal's nose and jaws.

neuter (NOO-tuhr) - to remove a male animal's reproductive glands.

nutrition - that which promotes growth, provides energy, repairs body tissues, and maintains life.

parti-color - having a dominant color broken up by patches of one or more other colors.

pregnant - having one or more babies growing within the body.

shed - to cast off hair, feathers, skin, or other coverings or parts by a natural process.

socialize - to accustom an animal or a person to spending time with others.

spay - to remove a female animal's reproductive organs.

vaccine (vak-SEEN) - a shot given to prevent illness or disease.

WEB SITES

To learn more about Pomeranians, visit ABDO Publishing Company online. Web sites about Pomeranians are featured on our Book Links page. These links are routinely monitored and updated to provide the most current information available.

www.abdopublishing.com

INDEX